*The publisher would like to thank the following for their*
*kind permission to use their photographs in this book:*

Page 8: © Skulls Unlimited; page 9: Seapics.com; page 14: © pbgalleries / Alamy; page 15: © geckophoto / iStockphoto; page 16: © Brandon Cole; page 17: © J. L. & Hubert M. L. Klein / Biosphoto / Peter Arnold Inc.; page 22: © Alaska Stock LLC / Alamy; page 23: © Brandon Cole; page 42 bottom image: © Juniors / SuperStock; page 43 bottom image: © AFP / Getty Images; page 44 top image: © www.skullsunlimited.com; page 45 top image: © www.skullsunlimited.com; page 46 center image: © Martin Zwick / age footstock / SuperStock; page 47 center image: © Victoria Stone & Mark Deeble / Getty Images; page 52 full-page image © Chokniti Khongchum / Shutterstock; page 53 full-page image: © vovol / Shutterstock; page 70: © Peter Larson / Corbis, Black Hills Institute of Geological Research, Inc., Hill City, South Dakota; page 71: © Loui Psihoyos / Corbis; page 72: © Ethan Miller / Getty Images; page 73: © Thierry Hubin, courtesy of Royal Belgian Institute of Natural Science Museum, Brussels; page 74: © Louie Psihoyos / Science Faction; page 75: © Barbara Strnadova / Photo Researchers, Inc.; page 112: © Lupa; page 113: © Jurgen & Christine Sohn FLPA; page 115: © Soren Andersson / WpN / Photoshot; page 118: top: © Daniel J. Cox / Photographer's Choice / Getty Images; bottom: © Chris Klinger; page 119: top: © Alecia Carter / ARKive; bottom: © Dave Watts / Visuals Unlimited, Inc.; page 127 full-page image: © FLPA / Alamy; page 132 bottom image: © Biosphoto / SuperStock; page 136 center image: © Werner Bollmann / Getty Images; page 137 center image © Charles McDougal / ardea.com; page 141 full-page image: © Michael & Patricia Fogden / Minden Pictures page 146 center image: © kool99 / istock; page 147 center image: © taolmor / istock.

*Thank you to my research assistants, Olivia Packenham and Will Harney.*
*To my pals Sean, Curran, and Marialice.*
*To T. rex Nancy and T. rex Alex and their little velociraptors, Brittany, Meaghan, Nick, and Tim.*
*To my pal Mark O'Connor . . . I have never heard of Mark Leonard.*
*To Luke Beaulieu, Jackson Pallotta, Quinn Cronin, and Elsie Girard.*

*—J.P.*

*Thank you to M C. Escher.*
*To my Tyrannaboyus rex — William.*
*To the Westwood Massachusetts High School Wolverines and Coach Russell Downes.*
*Dedicated to Mr. Andrew Wyeth.*

*—R.B.*

# -TABLE of CONTENTS-

# WHO WOULD WIN?

# KILLER WHALE
# VS.
# GREAT WHITE SHARK

What would happen if a killer whale met up with a great white shark? What if they had a fight? Who do you think would win?

Meet the killer whale, also known as an orca. It is a sea mammal. It breathes air through the blowhole on the top of its head. Just like you, killer whales have lungs. They hold their breath underwater.

BLOWHOLE

## KILLER WHALE NICKNAMES:
*BLACKFISH, ORCA, SEAWOLF,*
and
*KILLER OF WHALES*

Meet the great white shark. It's a huge fish that can't survive out of the water. Sharks and other fish don't breathe air. Fish get oxygen from water that flows through their gills.

**Like most sharks, the great white has five gill slits.**

**GREAT WHITE SHARK NICKNAMES:** *MAN-EATER, TOMMY, WHITE POINTER,* and *WHITE DEATH*

The killer whale has a huge jaw full of about fifty teeth. The teeth can be almost four inches long.

**DID YOU KNOW?**

*If the killer whale loses an adult tooth, it doesn't grow back.*

**ACTUAL SIZE**

*A killer whale tooth looks like this!*

A great white shark has a gigantic mouth full of several rows of razor-sharp teeth. It's scary just to look at them.

**DID YOU KNOW?**

If a shark loses a tooth, another tooth takes its place. During a shark's life, it can lose more than 3,000 teeth.

**ACTUAL SIZE**

A great white shark tooth looks like this!

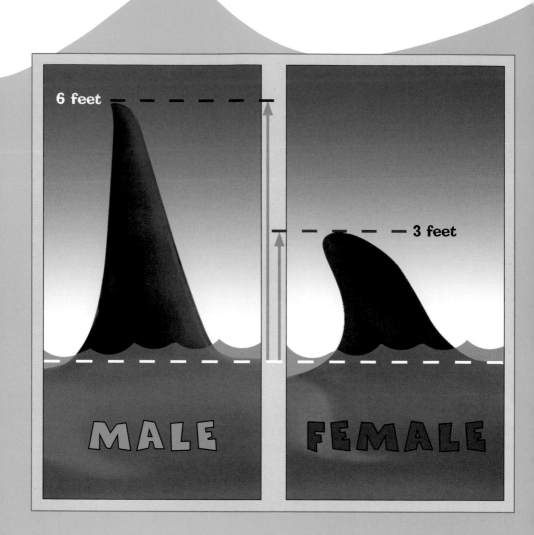

The killer whale's dorsal fin looks like these. On a male killer whale, the dorsal fin can be up to six feet tall.

Killer whales can be found in all oceans.

Male and female great white sharks have dorsal fins that look the same.

Great white sharks are also found in all oceans.

Killer whales are meat eaters. Their favorite foods are seals and sea lions, but they also eat salmon and other fish. A killer whale was once seen grabbing a moose and a deer off the shoreline!

The killer whale is king of the food chain. It has no natural enemies.

*The ocean is more like a food <u>web</u> than a food chain. In the ocean, everything eats almost everything else.*

Great white sharks eat fish,
but have also been known to eat
seals, sea lions, and even sea turtles.
Now and then, they eat a few people.

A great white shark is also high on the
food chain. It is the largest predatory fish.

*Tiny plankton is eaten
by small fish. Small fish get eaten by
bigger fish. Bigger fish get eaten
by larger fish, and so on.*

**MALE**

**23 feet**

**19 feet**

**FEMALE**

A male killer whale is bigger than a female killer whale.
A female is about four feet shorter.

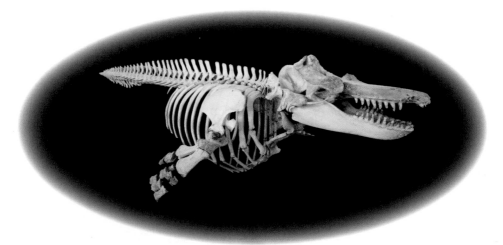

Killer whales have bones. This is a killer whale skeleton.

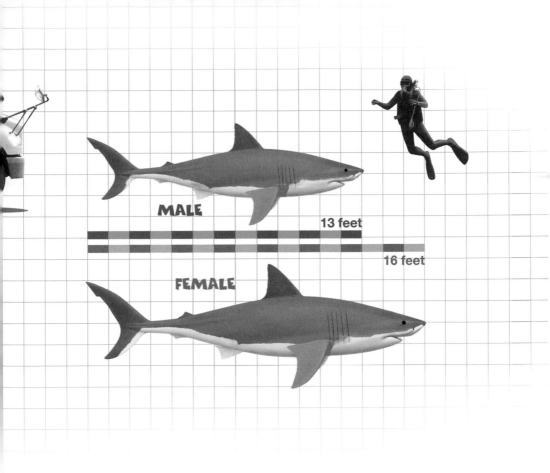

MALE

13 feet

16 feet

FEMALE

The female great white shark is bigger than the male. Females are wider and about three feet longer.

**LOOK! NO BONES!**

Great white sharks do not have bones. Shark skeletons are made of cartilage. Feel your own ear. It is made of cartilage.

Although they are huge, killer whales can jump completely out of the water.

**DID YOU KNOW?**

Killer whales might jump for fun, to knock some whale lice off their skin, or to catch a fish or a seal.

In a fight, who do you think would win? A killer whale or a great white shark?

Wow! Great white sharks can jump completely out of the water too!

So look at the facts! Who do you think has an advantage? Who would win?

Like other sea mammals, killer whales have a horizontal tail.

Like other sharks, a great white shark has a vertical tail.

# SONAR

Killer whales have no ears. They bounce sounds off of approaching fish. They use sonar to navigate, to locate other creatures in the ocean, and to find each other. They recognize echoes and other vibrations in the water. This is called echolocation.

**Bonus Fact!**

**SONAR**

is an acronym:
**SO**und
**N**avigation
**A**nd
**R**anging

DID YOU KNOW?
Submarines also use sonar, but nature had it first. Bats use sonar too!

*Underwater, you look like this to a killer whale.*

# SMELL

*Underwater, the great
white shark senses
your electricity.*

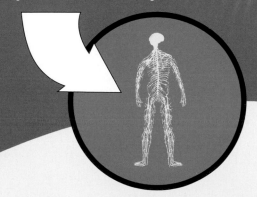

Great white sharks have a keen sense of smell.
They can also detect the electricity in fish and
other animals. They can tell if you are nervous.

Killer whales are family oriented. They live in groups called pods. Killer whale moms, dads, aunts, uncles, cousins, and kids eat, swim, and play together. They look out for each other.

Great white sharks are loners. Two and three have been seen hunting as a team. But mostly they travel, hunt, and eat alone.

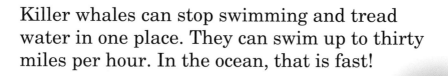

Killer whales can stop swimming and tread water in one place. They can swim up to thirty miles per hour. In the ocean, that is fast!

DID YOU KNOW?
Killer whales have smooth skin.

SPEED LIMIT 30

SPEED LIMIT 20

Great white sharks never stop swimming. Seawater must flow through their gills so they can get oxygen. They cruise along at about two miles per hour, but speed up in bursts to twenty miles per hour.

**Bonus Fact!**

*Great white sharks have rough skin. It is like sandpaper. Most fish have scales. Sharks have denticles. Denticles are like little tiny teeth on their skin.*

CLOSE-UP OF THE DENTICLES ON A GREAT WHITE'S SKIN

# Killer Whale Brain

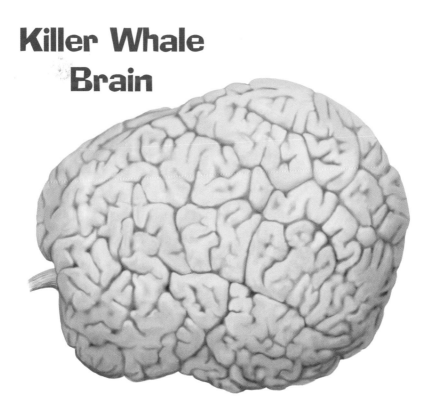

A killer whale's brain looks similar to a human brain, but is three times larger. Killer whales are extremely intelligent.

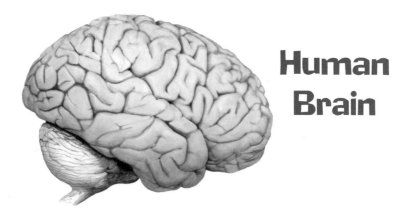

# Human Brain

# Great White Shark Brain

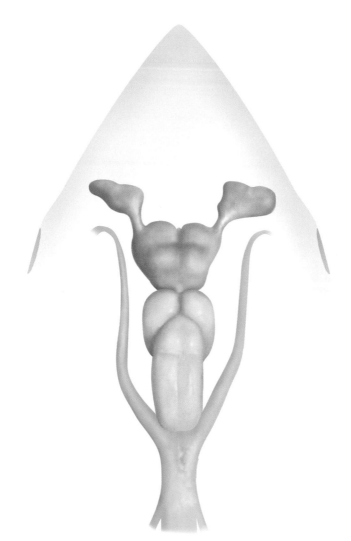

A great white shark does not have a round brain. It has different sections connected together. It is shaped like a letter "Y." Scientists think every section is connected to a different sense.

A killer whale can be captured, live in captivity, and trained to perform tricks. Killer whales are stars at aquariums and amusement parks.

Great white sharks have never been able to survive long in captivity. Hollywood loves to make movies about them. Great white sharks are movie stars!

FUN FACT:
*Jaws is one of the most popular movies of all time. For years, moviegoers were afraid to swim at the beach. Everyone knows the music: Dun! Dun! Dun! Dun! Dun! Dun!*

So, what would happen if a killer whale and a great white shark met in the ocean?

What if they were the same size?
What if they were both hungry?
What if they had a fight?

Uh-oh! They are in the same place at the same time! They sense each other. There is intense competition in nature. They are each planning their attacks!

Great white sharks like to attack from below. Killer whales like to attack from any side. They are getting closer. Then the fight happens.

# CRUNCH!

The great white shark makes the first move. It tries to attack with its sharp teeth. The killer whale outsmarts the shark and bites it. One! Two! Three seconds! The fight is over! It is no contest! The ferocious great white shark doesn't know what hit it.

The killer whale won today. What do you think will happen the next time a killer whale meets a great white shark? Who would win? Do you think the shark can overcome a killer whale's superior intelligence?

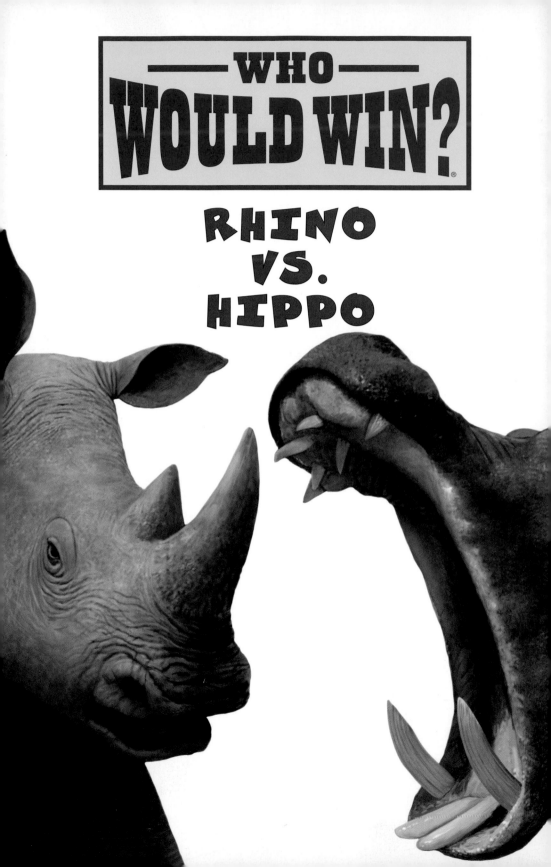

What would happen if a rhinoceros came face-to-face with a hippopotamus? What if they had a fight? Who do you think would win?

# MEET A RHINO

Rhino is a shortened version of rhinoceros, which means "nose horn." They certainly do have horns. This is a white rhino.

**FUN FACT**
*White rhinos cannot swim!*

**DID YOU KNOW?**
*The white rhino is the second-largest land mammal. Only elephants are bigger.*

Scientific name: *Ceratotherium simum.*

# MEET A HIPPO

Hippo is a shortened version of hippopotamus. Hippopotamus means "river horse." From now on, we will call them rhino and hippo.

**DEFINITION**
*A mammal is a warm-blooded animal with fur or hair that gives milk to its young.*

Scientific name: *Hippopotamus amphibius.*

# TYPES OF RHINOS

There are five species of rhinos.

## WHITE RHINO

> **LANGUAGE FACT**
> White rhino's name may have come from the Dutch word weid. It means "wide," as in wide lips.

> **COLOR FACT**
> White rhinos and black rhinos actually are both gray and look alike.

## INDIAN RHINO

## BLACK RHINO

> **HORN FACT**
> Indian and Javan rhinos have only one horn.

## JAVAN RHINO

## SUMATRAN RHINO

# TYPES OF HIPPOS

There are two species of hippos.

## HIPPOPOTAMUS

### HEIGHT FACT
*The pygmy hippo is half as tall as a hippopotamus.*

## PYGMY HIPPO

### DID YOU KNOW?
*The pygmy hippo weighs only one-fourth as much as a hippo.*

# WHITE RHINO TERRITORY

White rhinos live in Africa.

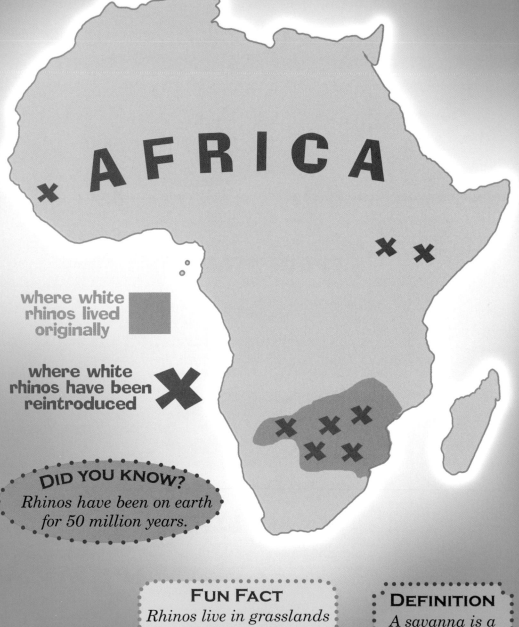

AFRICA

where white rhinos lived originally

where white rhinos have been reintroduced

**DID YOU KNOW?**
Rhinos have been on earth for 50 million years.

**FUN FACT**
Rhinos live in grasslands and savannas.

**DEFINITION**
A savanna is a grassy area with few trees.

# HIPPO TERRITORY

Hippos also live in Africa.

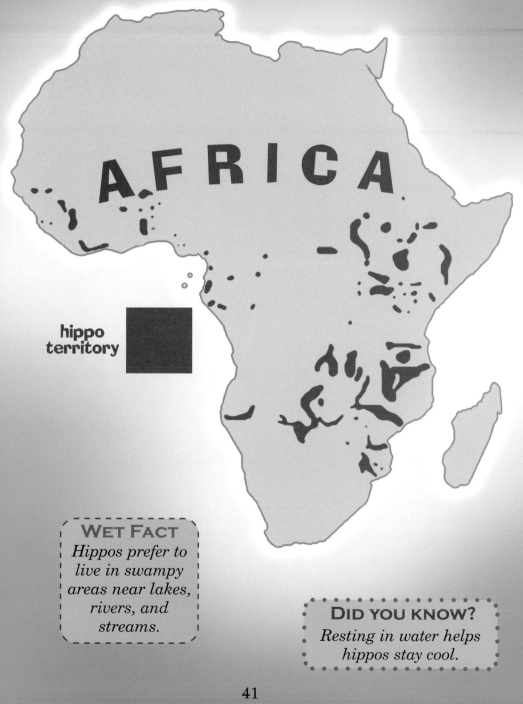

AFRICA

hippo territory

**WET FACT**
*Hippos prefer to live in swampy areas near lakes, rivers, and streams.*

**DID YOU KNOW?**
*Resting in water helps hippos stay cool.*

# RHINO DIET

White rhinos eat grass. Grass, grass, and more grass. Rhinos are not meat eaters; they have no interest in eating a hippo. White rhinos have wide lips. They pull up grass with their lips. They chew the grass with their back molars.

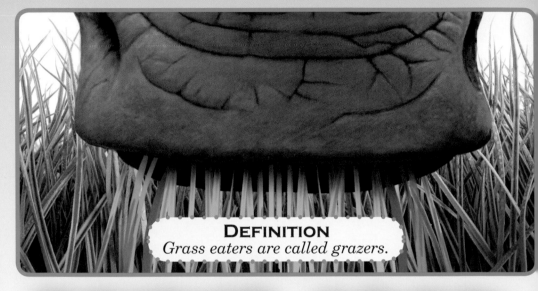

**DEFINITION**
*Grass eaters are called grazers.*

# RHINO BABY

This is a baby rhino.

**TUMMY FACT**
*A rhino has four sections to its stomach. It takes a lot to digest grass.*

**FUN FACT**
*When rhinos are born, they can weigh up to 90 pounds.*

# HIPPO DIET

Hippos also eat grass and some leaves. They prefer to eat at night. They rest during the day.

**FACT**
*Areas that have been eaten by hippos are called "hippo lawns."*

# HIPPO BABY

Which is cuter? A baby hippo or rhino?

**DID YOU KNOW?**
*A baby hippo weighs between 60–100 pounds.*

# RHINOCEROS SKELETON

A rhinoceros is a vertebrate animal. Vertebrates have backbones just like humans.

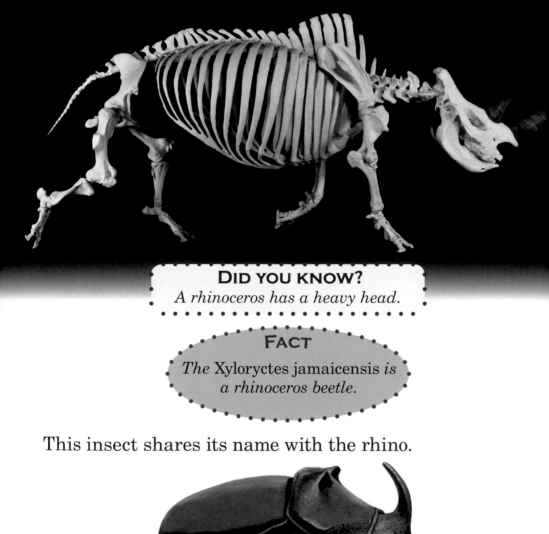

**DID YOU KNOW?**
*A rhinoceros has a heavy head.*

**FACT**
*The* Xyloryctes jamaicensis *is a rhinoceros beetle.*

This insect shares its name with the rhino.

# HIPPOPOTAMUS SKELETON

A hippo is also a vertebrate. Its spinal cord runs from its brain to its tail.

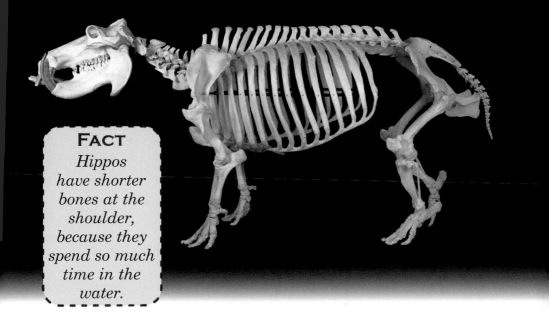

**FACT**
*Hippos have shorter bones at the shoulder, because they spend so much time in the water.*

This is a hippopotamus beetle.

**FACT?**
*The hippo beetle's scientific name is* Royis wandelirius.

**DID YOU KNOW?**
*One of the insects on these two pages is fake. Which one?*

# FREE RIDE

How would you like to ride around on a rhino? That is what oxpeckers do. These birds eat ticks, fleas, blood-sucking flies, and insect larvae off the backs of rhinos.

**GROSS FACT**
*Oxpeckers also eat earwax.*

**FUN FACT**
*Oxpeckers are also called tickbirds.*

**COLOR FACT**
*Oxpeckers are easy to recognize; they have red eyes and red beaks.*

Oxpeckers live only where there are larger mammals. They also like to ride on cattle, giraffes, zebra, and buffalo. Some scientists think it is a mutual relationship in which rhino and oxpecker both benefit. Others think the bird is a parasite.

# FREE CLEANING

The hippo loves the water. One reason might be the carp that clean its teeth, hide, and lips.

**LOVELY FACT**
*There is also a fish that follows hippos and eats their waste.*

**DEFINITION**
*A carp is a type of freshwater fish.*

**FACT**
*A hippo can hold its breath for five minutes.*

Hippos love freshwater, and so do humans. This sometimes creates conflicts between people and hippos.

# RHINO FOOT

A rhino foot has three toes.

**DID YOU KNOW?**
*An elephant foot has five toes.*

**Largest land mammal**

elephant

**Second-largest land mammal**

rhino

# HIPPO TOES

A hippo foot has four toes.

**FACT**
*A horse foot has one toe.*

Third-largest
land mammal

Largest mammal:
blue whale

hippo

human

# RHINO WEAPONS

A rhino's best weapon is its size. It is huge! Rhinos stand six feet high at the shoulders and weigh 8,000 pounds.

# 4 TONS

# HIPPO WEAPONS

The hippo's best weapons are its huge teeth and strong jaw. It has six big front teeth on its upper jaw and four teeth plus two long tusks on its lower jaw. It chews with its back molars.

## FACT
*Elephants, hippos, walrus, and wild boars have tusks.*

## DEFINITION
*A tusk is a long, pointed tooth. Tusks are usually found in pairs.*

# 3 TONS

A hippo's size is also a great weapon!

# RHINO SKIN

Rhinos are mammals but they have almost no hair.

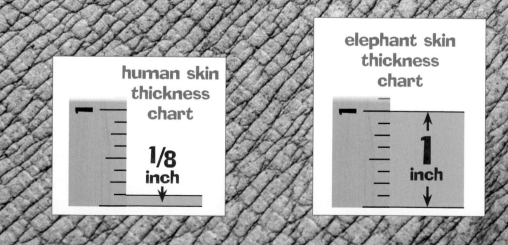

human skin
thickness
chart

**1/8**
inch

elephant skin
thickness
chart

**1**
inch

# HIPPO SKIN

Hippos also have almost no hair.

**IT'S NOT BLOOD!**
*Hippos have a natural skin lotion. Their skin oozes a reddish-orange oil.*

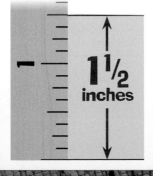

white rhino skin thickness chart

$1\frac{1}{2}$ inches

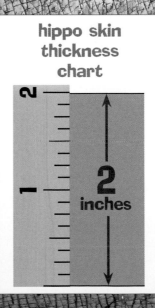

hippo skin thickness chart

2 inches

# I HEAR YOU

The rhino can swivel its ears in different directions. It has excellent hearing.

**DEFINITION**
*A group of rhinos is called a crash.*

**DID YOU KNOW?**
*A rhino can smell and hear a lion before it sees it.*

The hippo's head is beautifully designed. When swimming, its ears, nose, and eyes are above water. It is always on the lookout.

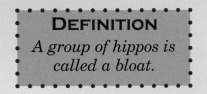

### DEFINITION
*A group of hippos is called a bloat.*

### DID YOU KNOW?
*A hippo can sleep underwater. While sleeping, it surfaces every five minutes to breathe.*

# RHINO SPEED

In short bursts, a rhino can run 30 miles per hour.

SPEED
LIMIT
30

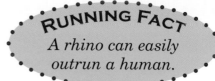

RUNNING FACT
*A rhino can easily
outrun a human.*

FUN FACT
*A rhinoceros can gallop
like a horse.*

# HIPPO SPEED

A hippo can run about 18 miles per hour. A hippo has no interest in running a marathon. It's not designed for long-distance running.

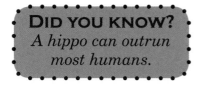

**DID YOU KNOW?**
*A hippo can outrun most humans.*

SPEED LIMIT **18**

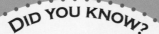

**DID YOU KNOW?**
*According to zoologists, the closest known relatives to hippos are dolphins and whales.*

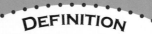

**DEFINITION**
*A zoologist is a scientist who studies animals and animal behavior.*

# LISTEN!

I told the illustrator not to show the rhino's rear end, but he did!

Dear Rob,
I don't think it's a good idea to show the rhino's rear end!
Jerry

**DID YOU KNOW?**
*The tail of a rhino has no significant function.*

# DON'T DO IT!

I asked the illustrator not to show the hippo's rear end, either!

**DID YOU KNOW?**
*From behind, the hippo and the rhino look similar.*

The hippo has a small tail. It's not long like a snow leopard tail, not fluffy like a horse tail, and not good for balance like a kangaroo tail.

The thirsty rhino walks over to the watering hole.

As the rhino takes a drink, the hippo opens its mouth and scares the rhino away. The thirsty rhino tries again. The hippo opens its big mouth, and the frightened rhino backs off.

Later, the hippo wants a drink. This time, the rhino charges and chases the hippo. The hippo returns. The rhino lowers its head and flashes its horns, and the hippo runs away.

Rhinos don't eat hippos. Hippos don't eat rhinos. But they are fighting for the same water.

Again the hippo opens its mouth, and the rhino runs away.

The rhino returns and charges the hippo. At the last second, the hippo turns around and opens its powerful jaws. The rhino retreats.

The rhino slowly walks back, with its head down and horns ready. The hippo swings around quickly and bites the rhino on its hind leg. Ouch! The rhino's leg is broken. It limps away.

The rhino has made a fatal mistake.

# WHO WOULD WIN?

# TYRANNOSAURUS REX VS. VELOCIRAPTOR

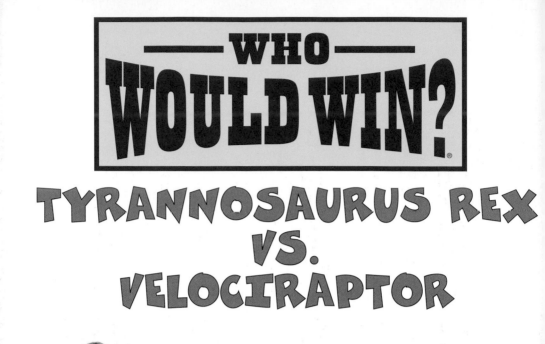

Author note:
T. rex and velociraptor lived on different
continents, millions of years apart. But what
might have happened if they met?

Let's go back millions of years.

What would happen if a Tyrannosaurus rex and a velociraptor met each other? What if both of these dinosaurs were hungry? What if they had a fight? Who do you think would win?

# PTEROSAURS

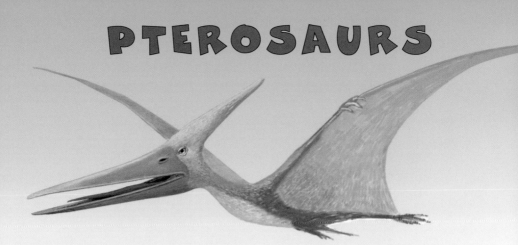

Millions of years ago, three types of huge creatures lived on earth. Pterosaurs flew in the sky.

# PLESIOSAURS

Plesiosaurs swam in the ocean.

# DINOSAURS

Dinosaurs walked on land.

**DEFINITION**
*Dinosaur means
"terrifying lizard."*

Some dinosaurs walked on two
legs, while others walked on four.

Today, pterosaurs, plesiosaurs, and dinosaurs are extinct,
which means they died out.

Meet Tyrannosaurus rex. It had a huge head, sharp teeth, big back legs, and teeny front arms. Just looking at one is scary! No one really knows what color it was. What do you think?

**FUN FACT**

*Lizards today come in many colors — some even can change color! Tyrannosaurus rex could have been almost any color.*

**QUESTION**
*Were they hot pink? Probably not!*

**WHAT IF?**
*Maybe they were green, like an iguana of today.*

## SCIENTIFIC NAME:
### Velociraptor means "speedy thief."
### Let's call him raptor.

Meet velociraptor. Paleontologists think it looked like this. Velociraptor scems to be built for speed and quick attack.

**FUN FACT**
*A paleontologist studies prehistoric life.*

**INTERESTING FACT**
*Prehistoric means "before recorded history."*

T. rex was discovered in modern times by people who found its fossils. Here is a photograph of the excavation site where this T. rex was found.

**DEFINITION**
*A fossil is the preserved remains of a dead plant or animal.*

**FUN FACT**
*The largest and most complete T. rex skeleton discovered is named Sue. It was found by and named after Sue Hendrickson, a paleontologist.*

Raptors were discovered the same way. Geologists and paleontologists found their fossilized bones.

This raptor fossil was found next to a protoceratops that it was fighting. Both dinosaurs died in this real-life "Who Would Win?"

Here is a full T. rex skeleton. When scientists assembled its fossilized bones, they learned that T. rex walked on two legs.

Here is a full raptor skeleton. Its fossilized bones look skinnier and more mobile than the T. rex skeleton.

T. rex had a huge jaw with more than fifty teeth. Its teeth were not designed for eating vegetables. It had carnivore teeth, as sharp as knives.

**DINO TRIVIA**
*When dinosaur fossils were first found in China, people thought they were ancient dragon bones.*

T. rex had a small brain. What did it think about?

The raptor also had a mouthful of sharp teeth. That means it was a meat eater, too.

**QUESTION**

*Would you want to be this dinosaur's dentist?*

**REMEMBER**

*Proportionally, a raptor has a larger brain than a T. rex.*

A raptor's teeth point inward to trap its prey.

Some scientists think that T. rex was a brutal hunter. It had the size, teeth, and design to be an apex predator. It is hard to believe that any animal would want to challenge a T. rex.

Other scientists think that T. rex was not aggressive, but was a carrion eater. Instead of hunting, it roamed for animals that were already dead.

The raptor was a predator that most likely hunted and ate smaller animals. It probably hunted in packs. Scientists think it hunted by ambushing its prey.

> **DEFINITION**
> *An ambush is an attack by surprise.*

*A group of raptors: Should we call them a bunch, a gang, a pack, a flock, a clique, a crash, a rumble, a storm, a herd, or something else?*

# T. REX FOOT

*Boom! Boom! Boom!* That is what a walking T. rex sounded like. The ground would shake, alerting nearby animals. *Boom! Boom! Boom!*

One toe
(horse)

Two toes
(sloth)

Three toes
(rhinoceros)

Four toes
(chicken)

Five toes
(human)

**QUESTION:**
*How is a T. rex like a chicken?*

**ANSWER:**
*They both have four toes on each foot.*

# RAPTOR FOOT

Paleontologists think the raptor was sneaky and quiet as it walked. A raptor probably tiptoed before attacking. It differs from other dinosaurs because it had a sickle on each foot.

## SICKLE THEORY #1

Did the raptor use its sickles to slash and cut its prey?

## SICKLE THEORY #2

Or were sickles used as grips to climb trees? Was the raptor a tree climber? What do you think?

# T. REX ARMS

The small arms of a T. rex seem almost useless. What could it do with them? A T. rex had only two fingers on each hand. In a football game, the T. rex would fumble the ball.

# RAPTOR ARMS

## GROSS FACT

*A raptor's arms and hands seem perfect for a dinosaur that is an aggressive hunter—quick, long, and strong. A raptor could easily rip apart its prey.*

Raptors had three fingers on each hand. The middle finger was the longest, and the first finger was the shortest.

# TYRANNOSAURUS REX TAIL

**DINO TRIVIA**

*The first dinosaur fossil ever discovered was named Megalosaurus.*

**INTERESTING FACT**

*T. rex walked on two legs, its tail balancing its body and huge head.*

The T. rex used its tail for balancing, but it may have also used it as a weapon. Getting whacked by its whip-tail could not have been fun.

# VELOCIRAPTOR TAIL

**DINOSAUR
TAILS**

**ANKYLOSAURUS**

CLUBBED

**POLACANTHUS**

JAGGED

**STEGOSAURUS**

SPIKED

Some dinosaur experts now think the raptor's tail may
have been straight and stiff.

They didn't look both ways before crossing the street.

They texted while driving.

One skateboard stunt too many.

Too many video games turned their brains to mush.

They liked to climb up trees, but didn't know how to climb down.

Aliens from other galaxies went hunting on earth and wiped out all of the dinosaurs.

# SCIENTIFIC THEORIES OF DINOSAUR EXTINCTION

## Asteroid Collision

A giant meteor hit earth and changed its climate.

## Rise of Small Animals

Small sneaky animals started eating dinosaur eggs faster than new eggs could be hatched.

## Food Chain Imbalance

The larger dinosaurs had trouble finding enough food and started eating each other.

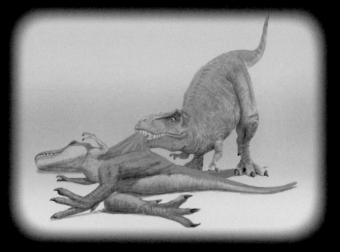

## Heavy Volcanic Activity

So much soot and dust erupted into the air that sunshine was blocked and plants died. The plant eaters didn't have enough to eat. Eventually the meat eaters had no plant eaters to eat.

## Ice Age
The earth became too cold.

## Disease
New infections, colds, and viruses attacked the dinosaurs.

What if a T. rex had a fight with a raptor? Who do you think would win?

Here comes a T. rex to face off with the raptor. It's not a fair fight. The T. rex is much bigger. But the raptor doesn't seem to be afraid. It does not run away. The raptor must have a secret.

Just as the T. rex is about to fight, the quick raptor leaps onto its back. The raptor slices the T. rex with its sickles. The angry T. rex bucks, and the raptor gets flung into the air.

## INTERESTING FACT

*A raptor was only about 3 to 4 feet high—not much taller than a third grader!*

The raptor gets right back up and jumps on the T. rex's tail. It slashes the T. rex but gets knocked to the ground again.

The raptor starts making a squeaking sound. The T. rex charges the little dinosaur. This time the T. rex is fed up. "Squeak! Squeak!" cries the raptor.

The raptor gets out its message. A pack of raptors comes to the rescue. The T. rex steps on one, then rips it with its teeth. But now the T. rex is in trouble.

What seemed like an easy fight has turned into a battle for survival. One, two, or even three raptors are no problem. But more than ten?

The raptor pack slashes and cuts the T. rex. It's over!
The T. rex crashes to the ground. It makes no sense to
fight a pack animal.

If it was a one-on-one fight, the huge T. rex would easily
beat a raptor. But nature doesn't always present a fair
fight.

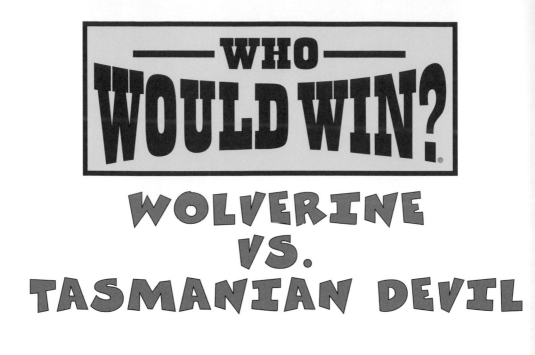

# WHO WOULD WIN?®

# WOLVERINE VS. TASMANIAN DEVIL

What would happen if a wolverine came face-to-face with a Tasmanian devil? What if they had a fight? Who do you think would win?

# SCIENTIFIC NAME OF
# WOLVERINE:
## "Gulo gulo"

Meet the wolverine. Its scientific name means "glutton." A glutton is someone who eats a lot.

**DEFINITION**
*A mammal is a warm-blooded animal with fur that gives milk to its young.*

**NICKNAMES**
*Skunk Bear, Nasty Cat, Carcajou, Quick Hatch, Gulon, and Mountain Cat.*

Wolverines are mammals. A wolverine is not a small wolf. It is in the weasel class of animals. A wolverine grows to be about three feet long, and weigh up to 40 pounds.

Meet the Tasmanian devil. Its scientific name means "flesh lover."

**DEFINITION**
*A marsupial is a mammal that carries its young in a pouch.*

**NICKNAMES**
*The Taz, the Butcher, Bear Devil.*

A Tasmanian devil is a type of mammal called a marsupial. It grows to be two and a half feet long and weigh up to 25 pounds.

# ANIMALS IN THE
# WEASEL FAMILY

ferret

cuscus

honey badger

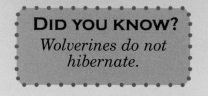

marten

least weasel

# OTHER MARSUPIALS

kangaroo

koala

## RARE FACT
*A yapok is an aquatic marsupial that lives in South America.*

wallaby

## THINK!
*Can you think of another animal that begins with Q?*

Page 157 has answers.

wombat

## FACT
*The Tasmanian wolf is an extinct marsupial.*

quoll

# NORTHERN HEMISPHERE

Wolverines live in cold climates, such as North America, Northern Asia, and Northern Europe. Wolverines love mountains, snow, ice, and glaciers.

**FACT**

*In deep snow, a wolverine has an advantage over prey that have hooves. Wolverine feet are wide.*

● wolverine territory

northern
hemisphere

southern
hemisphere

equator

**COLLEGE FACT**

*The University of Michigan teams call themselves the Wolverines.*

**DID YOU KNOW?**

*There are no wolverines in the southern hemisphere.*

# TASMANIA

Tasmanian devils live in Tasmania. Tasmania is an island off the southeast coast of Australia. They live in coastal scrubland and eucalyptus forests.

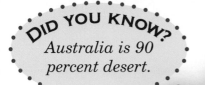

**DID YOU KNOW?**
*Australia is 90 percent desert.*

● Tasmanian devil's territory

AUSTRALIA

**GEOGRAPHY FACT**
*Tasmania used to be called Van Diemen's Land.*

TASMANIA

**SPORTS FACT**
*A soccer team from Bellerive, Tasmania, called itself the Tasmanian Devils Football Club.*

# WOLVERINE ADJECTIVES

## brutal
### tenacious
### ferocious
### solitary
### merciless
### mysterious
### elusive
### powerful
### volatile
### determined

## GOOD IDEA
Get a dictionary and look up these words!

# TASMANIAN DEVIL DESCRIPTIONS

loud

vicious

nasty

persistent

shy

relentless

fierce

## ANOTHER GOOD IDEA
Remember how to spell these words!

**CHALLENGE!**
*Get a thesaurus and look up similar words.*

# TEETH

Here is the skull of a wolverine. No one wants to get bitten by a wolverine. Look at the back teeth—they are perfect for crushing bones.

INCISOR

CANINE

CARNASSIAL

*Canine teeth are also called cuspids, eye teeth, and dog teeth.*

# JAWS

Here is the skull of a Tasmanian devil. When they bite, they don't like to let go.

**DENTAL FACT**
*Humans have no carnassials.*

**INCISOR**

**CANINE**

**CARNASSIAL**

Look at its jaws and teeth. My, what big incisors you have! It is a carnivore.

**DEFINITION**
*A carnivore is a meat eater.*

# BITE

If the wolverine and a great white shark were the same size, the wolverine would have a stronger jaw.

## Great White Shark

**FUN FACT**
*Great white shark teeth are not positioned tightly. They wiggle.*

## Wolverine

**DID YOU KNOW?**
*Scientists measure jaw strength by "bite force."*

# STRENGTH

If the Tasmanian devil and a tiger were the same size, the Tasmanian devil would have a stronger bite.

## Tiger

**AMAZING FACT**
*Tiger jaws are slightly larger than lion jaws.*

## Tasmanian Devil

**DID YOU KNOW?**
*The Tasmanian devil has the greatest bite-force ratio of any animal.*

# FAVORITE FOODS

A wolverine's favorite foods are most animals that live in its area. It eats rabbits, mice, sheep, caribou, lynx, and cows.

rabbit

mouse

sheep

caribou

cow

lynx

**FACT**
*A wolverine is a hunter but is also a scavenger.*

**MORE FAVORITE FOODS**
*Beaver, elk, badgers, otter, voles, dogs, cats, coyotes, squirrels, and chipmunks.*

**DEFINITION**
*A scavenger is an animal that eats already dead animals.*

# FAVORITE FOODS

The Tasmanian devil's favorite foods are wombats, possums, and wallabies.

wombat

wallaby

possum

# CLAWS

A wolverine has impressive claws. It has no problem digging dens, making snow caves, or shredding logs.

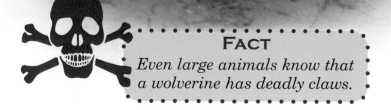

## FACT
*Even large animals know that a wolverine has deadly claws.*

# CLAWS

The Tasmanian devil also has long claws that are great for digging. Four claws point forward and one claw points to the side like a thumb. They can pick food up.

**DID YOU KNOW?**
*The Tasmanian devil has only four toes on each hind foot.*

**FUN FACT**
*A Tasmanian devil's hind legs are shorter than its front legs.*

# FUR

In North America, wolverines are a threatened species. Humans have slowly been moving into their territory, and wolverines need a lot of space. Wolverines have been hunted by fur trappers for hundreds of years. They have warm, beautiful fur.

The fur looks like this:

**DID YOU KNOW?**
*Wolverine fur was used for the lining in parkas.*

# TAIL

**CUTE FACT**
*A baby wolverine is called a kit.*

The tail of a wolverine is soft and fluffy. It does not protect it in a fight, but keeps it warm in sub-zero weather.

# FUR

Tasmanian devils are also an endangered species. There is no commercial market for Tasmanian devil fur. But Tasmanian devils were hunted for years because they killed animals that fur trappers wanted. They were considered pests.

The fur looks like this:

**CUTE FACT**
*A baby Tasmanian devil is called a joey.*

The Australian government paid people to kill Tasmanian devils. In 1930, the bounty for a dead Tasmanian devil was 25 cents.

# TAIL

**DEFINITION**
*A bounty is money paid for capturing or killing an animal.*

**FACT**
*Tasmanian devils have been protected since 1941.*

The Tasmanian devil stores fat in its tail. A Tasmanian devil with a skinny tail is an unhealthy animal.

# WOLVERINE LEGENDS

**BRRR !**

In sub-zero weather, a wolverine has no problem climbing up a steep icy mountain.

When tagged by scientists, wolverines were found to be able to hike 80 miles over hilly terrain in one day.

## QUESTION?

*How long would it take to drive 80 miles if you were traveling at 40 miles per hour?*

**ANSWER**
*2 hours.*

## ONE WOLVERINE CAN MAKE A PACK OF WOLVES RUN AWAY.

Wolverines are so ferocious that scientists only go near them after they have been tranquilized.

## DEFINITION

*Tranquilized means drugged by medicine. Zoologists and park rangers shoot drugs instead of bullets to make an animal sleep for a while.*

114

# TASMANIAN DEVIL LORE

Their scream has been described as horrifying.

# BOOK INTRUDER

The honey badger is mad. Why can't he be in this book? A honey badger can grab a cobra and rip its head off. It would not fear a wolverine or a Tasmanian devil. It wouldn't fear anything!

## NAME FACT
*The honey badger got its name by fearlessly charging headfirst into African killer bee hives.*

## DEFINITION
*An intruder is someone who goes into a place uninvited.*

**AFRICA**

## FACT
*The honey badger lives in Africa and in Asia.*

Should the honey badger get his own book? Which would you prefer reading?

## WOLVERINE VS. HONEY BADGER
### or
## HONEY BADGER VS. TASMANIAN DEVIL

# UH-OH!
# WHO'S THE TOUGHEST?

Three incredible animals! They all look somewhat similar.

**WOLVERINE**

In North America the wolverine is considered the toughest animal for its size.

**TASMANIAN DEVIL**

Many people from Australia say that, pound for pound, the Tasmanian devil is the toughest animal in the world. That is quite a compliment, because Australia and Tasmania have some of the most rugged animals on Earth.

**HONEY BADGER**

People in Africa say that the honey badger is the toughest animal. All three live on different continents. How could they ever meet?

# SPEED

A wolverine can run up to 30 miles per hour, which is faster than a human.

# TRAP

The safest way to catch a wolverine is with a log-box trap. A chunk of deer is great bait. If you do not check the trap within 24 hours, the wolverine will claw its way out of the trap.

**DID YOU KNOW?**
*A log-box trap doesn't hurt the wolverine.*

# SPEED

Tasmanian devils can run about 16 miles per hour.

SPEED LIMIT 16

# TRAP

The safest way to catch a Tasmanian devil is to set a PVC pipe trap. The Tasmanian devil crawls in to get at the bait. A steak would be great bait.

The wolverine and the Tasmanian devil meet. The Tasmanian devil lets out a scary screech.

The loud noise frightens the wolverine. He takes a step back. The wolverine is puzzled by the Tasmanian devil's scream.

Then the wolverine realizes the Tasmanian devil makes a lot of noise, but takes no action.

He charges at the Tasmanian devil, knocking him down. The wolverine swipes the Tasmanian devil's face.

The Tasmanian devil stops screaming. His face hurts. The wolverine claws at him again. They wrestle back and forth, trying to bite each other.

The wolverine has longer legs and claws. He scratches the Tasmanian devil again. Ouch!

The Tasmanian devil has trouble seeing. The wolverine bites him. The wolverine bites him again and again.

The wolverine wins. This time, the Tasmanian devil is no match for the wolverine.

# WHO WOULD WIN?

## ALLIGATOR VS. PYTHON

What would happen if an alligator had a fight with a python? Wow—these are two deadly reptiles! Who is the toughest? Who do you think would win?

# MEET THE ALLIGATOR

This is an American alligator. It can weigh up to 1,000 pounds. Scientific name: *Alligator mississippiensis*. These creatures live from Texas to North Carolina.

**FACT**
*Alligators are reptiles.*

**DEFINITION**
*Reptiles are cold-blooded animals that have dry scales. Snakes, crocodiles, lizards, and turtles are also reptiles.*

**BIG FACT**
*The American alligator is the largest reptile in North America.*

# MEET THE PYTHON

This is a Burmese python. Scientific name: *Python bivittatus*. The Burmese python can grow up to 19 feet long. People have seen them swallow a deer, a cat, and a pig. Yikes!

**FACT**
*Pythons are snakes.*
*Snakes are reptiles.*

**FANG FACT**
*Pythons are not venomous.*
*They have no poison.*

**ANCIENT FACT**
*Dinosaurs were also reptiles.*

# CROCODYLIA

There are four types of reptiles in an animal group called crocodylia.

**CROCODILE**

NOSE SHAPE
TOP VIEW

Crocodiles have a V-shaped head. When they close their mouths, you can see a long bottom tooth.

**ALLIGATOR**

NOSE SHAPE
TOP VIEW

Notice the wide head. When they close their wide mouths, you can't see the bottom teeth.

**GAVIAL**

NOSE SHAPE
TOP VIEW

Gavials have a narrow, pointy snout. Great for catching fish!

**CAIMAN**

NOSE SHAPE
TOP VIEW

The smallest crocodylian. A Cuvier's dwarf caiman is the smallest. All four types of crocodylia have lots of teeth!

We will use an American alligator to fight the Burmese python

# BIG SNAKES

The Burmese python is one of the five largest snakes in the world. Here are the other four:

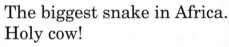

## RETICULATED PYTHON

The longest snake in the world. Yikes!

**LENGTH FACT**
*A reticulated python can be 30 feet long!*

## GREEN ANACONDA

The heaviest snake in the world. Wow!

**WEIGHT FACT**
*A green anaconda can weigh almost 600 pounds!*

## AFRICAN ROCK PYTHON

The biggest snake in Africa. Holy cow!

**DID YOU KNOW?**
*It can grow 20 feet long and weigh almost 200 pounds!*

## SCRUB PYTHON

Another huge snake! Cool.

**COLORFUL FACT**
*Snakes come in every color.*

### SNAKE NUMBERS

*There are about 3,000 known types of snakes in the world. Snakes have no arms and no legs. They have no moveable eyelids.*

# BEHAVE!

The American alligator lives in North Carolina, South Carolina, Georgia, Florida, Alabama, Mississippi, Louisiana, and Texas. Most of these are warm Gulf Coast states.

> **ICE FACT**
> *An alligator would freeze to death in Alaska.*

GULF COAST

**where alligators live** ◼

Alligators love water. They live in ponds, lakes, rivers, estuaries, swamps, marshlands, and bayous. They tolerate a little salt water, and brackish water, but they prefer freshwater.

# WE KNOW WHERE YOU LIVE!

The Burmese python lives in Southeast Asia. It got its name from Burma, which is now called Myanmar.

CHINA

BANGLADESH

INDIA

MYANMAR

LAOS

THAILAND

CAMBODIA

VIETNAM

**where Burmese pythons live**

MALAYSIA

BORNEO

INDONESIA

Oops! Some careless people let their pet Burmese pythons go in the Florida Everglades. Now the Everglades are overrun by pythons that don't belong here. They are an invasive species.

FLORIDA

### THE EVERGLADES
*A huge swampland full of water and tall grass in southern Florida.*

### DEFINITION
*An invasive species is a plant or animal that lives somewhere that is not their natural habitat. Invasive species usually cause damage and upset the balance of nature.*

# SORRY!

Sorry, saltwater crocodile, you are the biggest, heaviest, scariest, and meanest of all crocodiles. But you are too big for this book. Saltwater crocodiles live in Australia. We'll save you for another *Who Would Win?* book. How about: *Saltwater Crocodile vs. Mosquito?*

## SIZE FACT
*Saltwater crocodiles can grow up to 20 feet long!*

Here is an albino alligator.

## DEFINITION
*Albino means a lack of skin color.*

# YOU'RE OUT, TOO!

Here is the smallest snake in the world, the Barbados thread snake. It can't be in this book, either. Sorry, it's too small to fight the alligator.

**actual size**

## REPTILE FACT

*Some lizards—such as the island glass lizard—have no arms or legs. They may look like snakes, but they are legless lizards.*

## FACT

*A flowerpot snake is also small.*

Typical Burmese pythons have a color design similar to a giraffe. An albino Burmese python is mostly white but also has some color—usually light yellow and light orange.

# TEETH

Alligators have a huge, strong jaw full of big teeth.
They have about 80 teeth, which are powerful weapons.

## FACT
*An alligator's jaw has the bite strength equal to 2,000 pounds per square inch. No human can lift 2,000 pounds. That's a ton!*

## TEETH TYPE
*A dentist would say that alligators have conical-shaped teeth. Their teeth are shaped like an ice cream cone.*

# FANGS AND TEETH

Snakes don't chew their food. They have teeth designed to hold dinner. Slowly their strong, flexible jaws wiggle the food into their mouths, and they swallow it whole.

## GOOFY QUESTION
*Would you like to replace your teeth with a mouthful of fangs?*

## FANG TYPE
*Snake fangs are shaped like curved knives.*

Yikes! Burmese python teeth are sharp fangs that face inward. It is hard for an animal to escape the bite of a Burmese python.

# ROLL— A GREAT TACTIC!

When an alligator gets hold of an animal, it rolls. This twists the animal and often breaks its arms or legs. An alligator is so strong, it can roll and rip its prey's limb off.

The roll is an amazing move. How do alligators learn it? We can only wonder.

**NOT A FUN FACT**
*Yes, alligators have eaten a few people.*

**MIDNIGHT SNACK?**
*Alligators don't always eat the whole animal they catch. They often bury it and eat the rest later.*

# ENCIRCLE AND SQUEEZE, A DEADLY TECHNIQUE

Burmese pythons kill their prey by encircling them and squeezing them. They squeeze until the animal can't breathe.

**OH NO!**
*Yes, Burmese pythons have eaten a few people.*

**DEFINITION**
*Snakes that squeeze their prey are called constrictors.*

**WARNING**
*Don't ever let someone put a python around your neck or on your shoulders.*

137

# ALLIGATOR TAIL

The alligator has a long, thick tail. The tail is almost as long as the rest of its body. It uses the tail to steer and swim.

**SPEED LIMIT 30**

WHACK!

**SPEED FACT**

*Alligators can only run 30 miles per hour for a short distance.*

**DID YOU KNOW?**

*The alligator can also smack you with its tail.*

Alligators are excellent swimmers. They can swim at 10 miles per hour.

# DO SNAKES HAVE TAILS?

Not really. Its whole body is just shaped like a tail. Pythons are also excellent swimmers.

**FACT**
*Burmese pythons have about 4,000 muscles.*

Burmese pythons are faster in the water. They can swim at 5 miles per hour.

# HIDDEN

Can you find the alligator? He is well disguised in this swamp. The alligator patiently waits with his nose and eyes above water.

**FACT**
*Alligators cannot breathe underwater.*

**DID YOU KNOW?**
*Underwater, alligators close their nose and ears.*

**BONUS FACT**
*Usually an alligator holds its breath underwater for about 15 minutes.*

Alligators have been known to hold their breath for up to an hour. In cold water, an alligator can hold its breath even longer.

**QUESTION**
*Can alligators climb trees?*

# CAMOUFLAGED

The Burmese python is also well disguised. It looks like leaves on the ground.

**DID YOU KNOW?**
*The python also holds its eyes and nose above water.*

**LUNG FACT**
*A Burmese python can hold its breath underwater for at least a half hour.*

Beware! Burmese pythons can climb trees.

**THANK GOODNESS!**
*Alligators can't climb trees.*

# FOOD

Alligators eat insects, snails, fish, turtles, and other reptiles when they are young. As an alligator gets older, they eat larger creatures. A young alligator might get eaten by a big fish, hawk, or eagle. Hatchlings, watch out!

## DEFINITION
A baby alligator is called a hatchling. Hatchlings eat insects and shrimp.

## OLD
A grown-up alligator often goes out of the water to grab a huge mammal like a dog, a cow, or a horse.

## FACT
Alligators are good at sneaking up on birds. They have been known to eat a duck, a goose, or an egret.

# LET'S EAT

A Burmese python eats anything it can swallow whole. A python can unhinge its jaw, stretch its ligaments, and swallow something bigger than its mouth, usually small mammals, frogs, and birds.

**FACT**

*A python can taste, smell, and tell the temperature with its tongue.*

# PEOPLE EAT ALLIGATORS!

Some people eat alligators. You might find these menu items in some US Gulf Coast states:

## Today's Specials

### GRILLED ALLIGATOR STEAK

*Juicy charcoal-broiled alligator steak, lightly seasoned, served with grits and fresh beet greens.*

### ALLIGATOR FINGERS AND FRENCH FRIES

*Lightly breaded, deep-fried alligator strips, cooked until golden brown, served with crispy french fries.*

### BBQ ALLIGATOR

*Slow-smoked gator fillets, dressed with our famous barbecue sauce, with creamy mashed potatoes, and choice of vegetable or crisp garden salad.*

### ALLIGATOR SAUSAGES

*Hand-stuffed, ground alligator, seasoned with hot spices, served over rice, with roasted red pepper, sweet onion, and dijon mustard.*

# PEOPLE EAT PYTHONS, TOO!

Americans do not usually eat pythons. But some of us eat other snakes, such as rattlesnake. In other parts of the world people eat pythons. They say it is delicious.

**DID YOU KNOW?**
*There is a restaurant in Florida that serves python pizza. They also offer frog leg pizza.*

QUESTION
*Has any chef ever made python ice cream, python cake, or chocolate-covered python? We don't know!*

# ALLIGATOR SKIN

Many products are made from alligator skin. They include cowboy boots, belts, shoes, pants, and car seat covers.

**ROUGH FACT**
*People say that an alligator's back skin feels like a bumpy truck tire.*

*Mirror, mirror, on the wall, who is the coolest reptile of all?*

**BELLY FACT**
*The alligator's belly skin is smooth.*

**DID YOU KNOW?**
*There is a fish called an alligator gar.*

# BURMESE PYTHON SKIN

Snakes have smooth, rugged skin. You can often identify a snake by the color and design of its skin.

**FACT**
*Snakes are not slimy.*
*They have dry, scaly skin.*

*Everglades alligator, you're not persuasive. I'll soon be king because I'm invasive.*

**DID YOU KNOW?**
*Snakes molt. As they grow larger, they shed their clear outer skin, usually in one piece.*

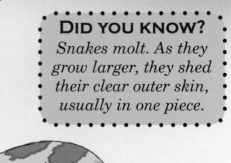

# I SEE YOU

Alligators have excellent eyesight.

# FEET

Alligators have strong legs, tough ugly feet, and long nails. They are great at digging holes to bury uneaten food, or dig pools of water.

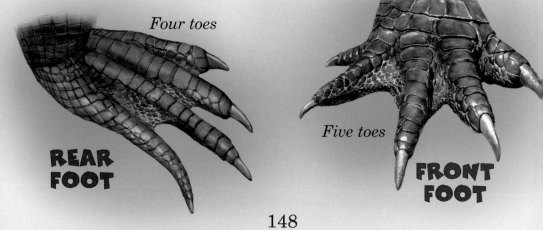

*Four toes*

*Five toes*

**REAR FOOT**

**FRONT FOOT**

# I SENSE YOU

Python brains see a visual world and a thermal world.

# NO FEET

Snakes don't have feet. Snakes slither along the ground on their wide belly scales.

*python belly scales*
**BOTTOM VIEW**

A Burmese python and an alligator meet each other in the Florida Everglades.

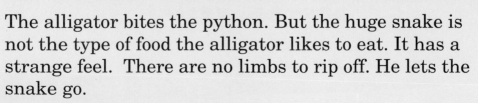

The alligator bites the python. But the huge snake is not the type of food the alligator likes to eat. It has a strange feel.  There are no limbs to rip off. He lets the snake go.

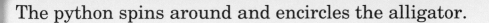

The fight takes a long time. The snake starts squeezing the alligator. The alligator flips and tries to roll away.

The alligator tries to bite. The python slips away. After a long battle back and forth, the alligator gets tired.

The snake circles the alligator, then unhinges its jaw and starts swallowing the alligator. The python's strong jaw and throat muscles keep on pulling in the alligator.

The alligator can't breathe. The snake swallows the head. Then it swallows the alligator's body. Its legs are rugged and tough to eat.

The python finally gets the alligator's tail in its mouth. It's an ugly sight. The alligator is dead. The python has a bellyache. It will take a month for the python to digest it. But the python won this fight.

# WHO HAS THE ADVANTAGE? CHECKLIST

**KILLER WHALE**                    **GREAT WHITE SHARK**

| Killer Whale | | Great White Shark |
|:---:|:---:|:---:|
| ☐ | Breathing | ☐ |
| ☐ | Teeth | ☐ |
| ☐ | Dorsal fin | ☐ |
| ☐ | Size | ☐ |
| ☐ | Tail | ☐ |
| ☐ | Smell | ☐ |
| ☐ | Vision | ☐ |
| ☐ | Family | ☐ |
| ☐ | Intelligence | ☐ |
| ☐ | Speed | ☐ |

Author note: This is one way the fight might have ended.
How would you write the ending?

# WHO HAS THE ADVANTAGE?
## CHECKLIST

**RHINO**            **HIPPO**

| RHINO | | HIPPO |
|:---:|:---:|:---:|
| ☐ | Weight | ☐ |
| ☐ | Size | ☐ |
| ☐ | Weapons | ☐ |
| ☐ | Skin | ☐ |
| ☐ | Ears | ☐ |
| ☐ | Swimming ability | ☐ |
| ☐ | Speed | ☐ |

Author note: This is one way the fight might have ended.
How would you write the ending?

# WHO HAS THE ADVANTAGE?
## CHECKLIST

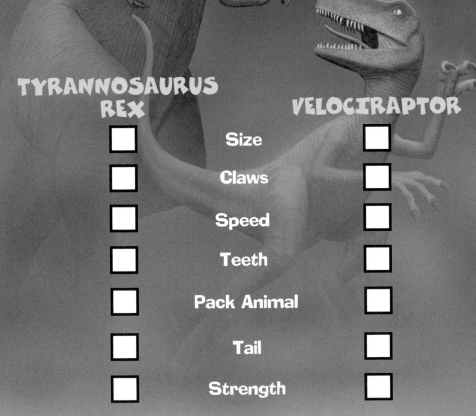

| TYRANNOSAURUS REX | | VELOCIRAPTOR |
|:---:|:---:|:---:|
| ☐ | Size | ☐ |
| ☐ | Claws | ☐ |
| ☐ | Speed | ☐ |
| ☐ | Teeth | ☐ |
| ☐ | Pack Animal | ☐ |
| ☐ | Tail | ☐ |
| ☐ | Strength | ☐ |

Author note: This is one way the fight might have ended. How would you write the ending?

# WHO HAS THE ADVANTAGE? CHECKLIST

The honey badger is still mad he is not in this book. Can you help him grade these two magnificent animals? Who has the advantage?

| WOLVERINE | | TASMANIAN DEVIL |
|:---:|:---:|:---:|
| ☐ | Size | ☐ |
| ☐ | Length | ☐ |
| ☐ | Jaw strength | ☐ |
| ☐ | Voice | ☐ |
| ☐ | Fur | ☐ |
| ☐ | Claws | ☐ |

Author note: This is one way the fight might have ended. How would you write the ending?

## PAGE 99 ANSWERS:

*Quagga: extinct zebra; Quahog: clam; Quail: bird; Quarter horse; Quokka: Australian marsupial; Quoll: marsupial from Australia and New Guinea*

# WHO HAS THE ADVANTAGE?

## CHECKLIST

| ALLIGATOR | | BURMESE PYTHON |
|:---:|:---:|:---:|
| ☐ | Size | ☐ |
| ☐ | Teeth or Fangs | ☐ |
| ☐ | Camouflage | ☐ |
| ☐ | Eyesight | ☐ |
| ☐ | Tactics | ☐ |
| ☐ | Speed | ☐ |
| ☐ | Skin | ☐ |

Author note: This is one way the fight might have ended. How would you write the ending?

158

# WHO DO YOU THINK WOULD WIN?

**Find out who comes out on top by reading more of these animal matchups!**